THE STRANGER

Albert Camus

This edition published by Spark Publishing

Spark Publishing
A Division of SparkNotes LLC
120 Fifth Avenue, 8th Floor
New York, NY 10011

Printed and bound in the United States

ISBN 1-58663-453-4

INTRODUCTION: STOPPING TO BUY SPARKNOTES ON A SNOWY EVENING

Whose words these are you *think* you know.
Your paper's due tomorrow, though;
We're glad to see you stopping here
To get some help before you go.

Lost your course? You'll find it here.
Face tests and essays without fear.
Between the words, good grades at stake:
Get great results throughout the year.

Once school bells caused your heart to quake
As teachers circled each mistake.
Use SparkNotes and no longer weep,
Ace every single test you take.

Yes, books are lovely, dark, and deep,
But only what you grasp you keep,
With hours to go before you sleep,
With hours to go before you sleep.

CONTENTS

NOTE: This SparkNote refers to the Vintage International edition of *The Stranger*, translated by Matthew Ward from the French. Other translations of the novel vary.

Context

LBERT CAMUS WAS BORN on November 7, 1913, in French colonial Algeria. In 1914, his father was killed in World War I, at the Battle of the Marne. Albert, his mother, and his brother shared a two-bedroom apartment with the family's maternal grandmother and a paralyzed uncle. Despite his family's extreme poverty, Camus attended the University of Algiers, supporting his education by working a series of odd jobs. However, one of several severe attacks of tuberculosis forced him to drop out of school. The poverty and illness Camus experienced as a youth greatly influenced his writing.

After dropping out of the university, Camus eventually entered the world of political journalism. While working for an anti-colonialist newspaper, he wrote extensively about poverty in Algeria. From 1935 to 1938, Camus ran the Théâtre de l'Equipe, an organization that attempted to attract working-class audiences to performances of great dramatic works. During World War II, Camus went to Paris and became a leading writer for the anti-German resistance movement. He was also the editor of *Combat,* an important underground newspaper.

While in wartime Paris, Camus developed his philosophy of the absurd. A major component of this philosophy was Camus's assertion that life has no rational or redeeming meaning. The experience of World War II led many other intellectuals to similar conclusions. Faced with the horrors of Hitler's Nazi regime and the unprecedented slaughter of the War, many could no longer accept that human existence had any purpose or discernible meaning. Existence seemed simply, to use Camus's term, absurd.

The Stranger, Camus's first novel, is both a brilliantly crafted story and an illustration of Camus's absurdist world view. Published in 1942, the novel tells the story of an emotionally detached, amoral young man named Meursault. He does not cry at his mother's funeral, does not believe in God, and kills a man he barely knows without any discernible motive. For his crime, Meursault is deemed a threat to society and sentenced to death. When he comes to accept the "gentle indifference of the world," he finds peace with himself and with the society that persecutes him.

Camus's absurdist philosophy implies that moral orders have no rational or natural basis. Yet Camus did not approach the world with moral indifference, and he believed that life's lack of a "higher" meaning should not necessarily lead one to despair. On the contrary, Camus was a persistent humanist. He is noted for his faith in man's dignity in the face of what he saw as a cold, indifferent universe.

In 1942, the same year that *The Stranger* was published, Camus also published *The Myth of Sisyphus*, his famous philosophical essay on the absurd. These two works helped establish Camus's reputation as an important and brilliant literary figure. Over the course of his career he produced numerous novels, plays, and essays that further developed his philosophy. Among his most notable novels are *The Plague*, published in 1947, and *The Fall*, published in 1956. Along with *The Myth of Sisyphus*, *The Rebel* stands as his best-known philosophical essay. In recognition of his contribution to French and world literature, Camus was awarded the Nobel Prize for Literature in 1957. Tragically, he died in an automobile accident just three years later.

In the midst of the widespread intellectual and moral bewilderment that followed World War II, Camus's was a voice advocating the values of justice and human dignity. Though his career was cut short, he remains one of the most influential authors of the twentieth century, regarded both for the quality of his fiction and for the depth and insightfulness of his philosophy.

CAMUS, EXISTENTIALISM, AND *THE STRANGER*

The Stranger is often referred to as an "existential" novel, but this description is not necessarily accurate. The term "existentialism" is a broad and far-reaching classification that means many different things to many different people, and is often misapplied or overapplied. As it is most commonly used, existentialism refers to the idea that there is no "higher" meaning to the universe or to man's existence, and no rational order to the events of the world. According to this common definition of existentialism, human life is not invested with a redemptive or affirming purpose—there is nothing beyond man's physical existence.

Some ideas in *The Stranger* clearly resemble this working definition of existentialism, but the broader philosophy of existentialism includes aspects far beyond this definition that are not present in

The Stranger. Moreover, Camus himself rejected the application of the "existential" label to *The Stranger.* Hence, this SparkNote approaches *The Stranger* from the philosophical perspective of the absurd. "The absurd" is a term Camus himself coined, and a philosophy that he himself developed. Reading *The Stranger* with Camus's philosophy of the absurd in mind sheds a good deal of light on the text.

Although Camus's philosophical ideas resonate strongly within the text, it is important to keep in mind that *The Stranger* is a novel, not a philosophical essay. When reading the novel, character development, plot, and prose style demand just as much attention as the specifics of the absurd. This SparkNote only discusses the absurd when such discussion provides insight on the text. Otherwise, the focus of this SparkNote remains on the text itself, as with any great work of literature.

PLOT OVERVIEW

MEURSAULT, THE NARRATOR, is a young man living in Algiers. After receiving a telegram informing him of his mother's death, he takes a bus to Marengo, where his mother had been living in an old persons' home. He sleeps for almost the entire trip. When he arrives, he speaks to the director of the home. The director allows Meursault to see his mother, but Meursault finds that her body has already been sealed in the coffin. He declines the caretaker's offer to open the coffin.

That night, Meursault keeps vigil over his mother's body. Much to his displeasure, the talkative caretaker stays with him the whole time. Meursault smokes a cigarette, drinks coffee, and dozes off. The next morning, before the funeral, he meets with the director again. The director informs him that Thomas Perez, an old man who had grown very close to Meursault's mother, will be attending the funeral service. The funeral procession heads for the small local village, but Perez has difficulty keeping up and eventually faints from the heat. Meursault reports that he remembers little of the funeral. That night, he happily arrives back in Algiers.

The next day, Meursault goes to the public beach for a swim. There, he runs into Marie Cardona, his former co-worker. The two make a date to see a comedy at the movie theater that evening. After the movie they spend the night together. When Meursault wakes up, Marie is gone. He stays in bed until noon and then sits on his balcony until evening, watching the people pass on the street.

The following day, Monday, Meursault returns to work. He has lunch with his friend Emmanuel and then works all afternoon. While walking upstairs to his apartment that night, Meursault runs into Salamano, an old man who lives in his building and owns a mangy dog. Meursault also runs into his neighbor, Raymond Sintes, who is widely rumored to be a pimp. Raymond invites Meursault over for dinner. Over the meal, Raymond recounts how he beat up his mistress after he discovered that she had been cheating on him. As a result, he got into a fight with her brother. Raymond now wants to torment his mistress even more, but he needs Meursault to write a letter to lure his mistress back to him. Meursault agrees and writes the letter that night.

The following Saturday, Marie visits Meursault at his apartment. She asks Meursault if he loves her, and he replies that "it didn't mean anything," but probably not. The two then hear shouting coming from Raymond's apartment. They go out into the hall and watch as a policeman arrives. The policeman slaps Raymond and says that he will be summoned to the police station for beating up his mistress. Later, Raymond asks Meursault to testify on his behalf, and Meursault agrees. That night, Raymond runs into Salamano, who laments that his dog has run away.

Marie asks Meursault if he wants to marry her. He replies indifferently but says that they can get married if she wants to, so they become engaged. The following Sunday, Meursault, Marie, and Raymond go to a beach house owned by Masson, one of Raymond's friends. They swim happily in the ocean and then have lunch. That afternoon, Masson, Raymond, and Meursault run into two Arabs on the beach, one of whom is the brother of Raymond's mistress. A fight breaks out and Raymond is stabbed. After tending to his wounds, Raymond returns to the beach with Meursault. They find the Arabs at a spring. Raymond considers shooting them with his gun, but Meursault talks him out of it and takes the gun away. Later, however, Meursault returns to the spring to cool off, and, for no apparent reason, he shoots Raymond's mistress's brother.

Meursault is arrested and thrown into jail. His lawyer seems disgusted at Meursault's lack of remorse over his crime, and, in particular, at Meursault's lack of grief at his mother's funeral. Later, Meursault meets with the examining magistrate, who cannot understand Meursault's actions. The magistrate brandishes a crucifix and demands that Meursault put his faith in God. Meursault refuses, insisting that he does not believe in God. The magistrate cannot accept Meursault's lack of belief, and eventually dubs him "Monsieur Antichrist."

One day, Marie visits Meursault in prison. She forces herself to smile during the visit, and she expresses hope that Meursault will be acquitted and that they will get married. As he awaits his trial, Meursault slowly adapts to prison life. His isolation from nature, women, and cigarettes torments him at first, but he eventually adjusts to living without them, and soon does not even notice their absence. He manages to keep his mind occupied, and he sleeps for most of each day.

Meursault is taken to the courthouse early on the morning of his trial. Spectators and members of the press fill the courtroom. The subject of the trial quickly shifts away from the murder to a general discussion of Meursault's character, and of his reaction to his mother's death in particular. The director and several other people who attended the vigil and the funeral are called to testify, and they all attest to Meursault's lack of grief or tears. Marie reluctantly testifies that the day after his mother's funeral she and Meursault went on a date and saw a comedic movie. During his summation the following day, the prosecutor calls Meursault a monster and says that his lack of moral feeling threatens all of society. Meursault is found guilty and is sentenced to death by beheading.

Meursault returns to prison to await his execution. He struggles to come to terms with his situation, and he has trouble accepting the certainty and inevitability of his fate. He imagines escaping and he dreams of filing a successful legal appeal. One day, the chaplain comes to visit against Meursault's wishes. He urges Meursault to renounce his atheism and turn to God, but Meursault refuses. Like the magistrate, the chaplain cannot believe that Meursault does not long for faith and the afterlife. Meursault suddenly becomes enraged, grabs the chaplain, and begins shouting at him. He declares that he is correct in believing in a meaningless, purely physical world. For the first time, Meursault truly embraces the idea that human existence holds no greater meaning. He abandons all hope for the future and accepts the "gentle indifference of the world." This acceptance makes Meursault feel happy.

Character List

Meursault The protagonist and narrator of *The Stranger,* to whom the novel's title refers. Meursault is a detached figure who views and describes much of what occurs around him from a removed position. He is emotionally indifferent to others, even to his mother and his lover, Marie. He also refuses to adhere to the accepted moral order of society. After Meursault kills a man, "the Arab," for no apparent reason, he is put on trial. However, the focus of Meursault's murder trial quickly shifts away from the murder itself to Meursault's attitudes and beliefs. Meursault's atheism and his lack of outward grief at his mother's funeral represent a serious challenge to the morals of the society in which he lives. Consequently, society brands him an outsider.

Marie Cardona A former co-worker of Meursault who begins an affair with him the day after his mother's funeral. Marie is young and high-spirited, and delights in swimming and the outdoors. Meursault's interest in Marie seems primarily the result of her physical beauty. Marie does not seem to understand Meursault, but she feels drawn to Meursault's peculiarities nevertheless. Even when Meursault expresses indifference toward marrying her, she still wants to be his wife, and she tries to support him during his arrest and trial.

Raymond Sintes A local pimp and Meursault's neighbor. Raymond becomes angry when he suspects his mistress is cheating on him, and in his plan to punish her, he enlists Meursault's help. In contrast to Meursault's calm detachment, Raymond behaves with emotion and initiative. He is also violent, and beats his mistress as well as the two Arabs on the beach, one of whom is his mistress's brother. Raymond seems to be using

Meursault, whom he can easily convince to help him in his schemes. However, that Raymond tries to help Meursault with his testimony during the trial shows that Raymond does possess some capacity for loyalty.

Meursault's Mother Madame Meursault's death begins the action of the novel. Three years prior, Meursault sent her to an old persons' home. Meursault identifies with his mother and believes that she shared many of his attitudes about life, including a love of nature and the capacity to become accustomed to virtually any situation or occurrence. Most important, Meursault decides that, toward the end of her life, his mother must have embraced a meaningless universe and lived for the moment, just as he does.

The Chaplain A priest who attends to the religious needs of condemned men, the chaplain acts as a catalyst for Meursault's psychological and philosophical development. After Meursault is found guilty of premeditated murder and sentenced to death, he repeatedly refuses to see the chaplain. The chaplain visits Meursault anyway, and nearly demands that he take comfort in God. The chaplain seems threatened by Meursault's stubborn atheism. Eventually, Meursault becomes enraged and angrily asserts that life is meaningless and that all men are condemned to die. This argument triggers Meursault's final acceptance of the meaninglessness of the universe.

Thomas Perez One of the elderly residents at the old persons' home where Meursault's mother lived. Before Madame Meursault's death, she and Perez had become so inseparable that the other residents joked that he was her fiancé. Perez's relationship with Madame Meursault is one of the few genuine emotional attachments the novel depicts. Perez, as someone who expresses his love for Madame Meursault, serves as a foil the indifferent narrator.

CHARACTER LIST

The Examining Magistrate The magistrate questions Meursault several times after his arrest. Deeply disturbed by Meursault's apparent lack of grief over his mother's death, the magistrate brandishes a crucifix at Meursault and demands to know whether he believes in God. When Meursault reasserts his atheism, the magistrate states that the meaning of his own life is threatened by Meursault's lack of belief. The magistrate represents society at large in that he is threatened by Meursault's unusual, amoral beliefs.

The Caretaker A worker at the old persons' home where Meursault's mother spent the three years prior to her death. During the vigil Meursault holds before his mother's funeral, the caretaker chats with Meursault in the mortuary. They drink coffee and smoke cigarettes next to the coffin, gestures that later weigh heavily against Meursault as evidence of his monstrous indifference to his mother's death. It is peculiar that the court does not consider the caretaker's smoking and coffee drinking in the presence of the coffin to be similarly monstrous acts.

The Director The manager of the old persons' home where Meursault's mother spent her final three years. When Meursault arrives to keep vigil before his mother's funeral, the director assures him that he should not feel guilty for having sent her to the home. However, by raising the issue, the director implies that perhaps Meursault *has* done something wrong. When Meursault goes on trial, the director becomes suddenly judgmental. During his testimony, he casts Meursault's actions in a negative light.

Celeste The proprietor of a café where Meursault frequently eats lunch. Celeste remains loyal to Meursault during his murder trial. He testifies that Meursault is an honest, decent man, and he states that bad luck led Meursault to kill the Arab. Celeste's assertion that the murder had no rational cause and was simply a case of bad luck reveals a worldview similar to Meursault's.

Masson   One of Raymond's friends, who invites Raymond, Meursault, and Marie to spend a Sunday at his beach house with him and his wife. It is during this ill-fated trip to Masson's beach house that Meursault kills the Arab. Masson is a vigorous, seemingly contented figure, and he testifies to Meursault's good character during Meursault's trial.

The Prosecutor The lawyer who argues against Meursault at the trial. During his closing arguments, the prosecutor characterizes Meursault as a cool, calculating monster, using Meursault's lack of an emotional attachment to his mother as his primary evidence. He demands the death penalty for Meursault, arguing that Meursault's moral indifference threatens all of society and therefore must be stamped out.

Salamano One of Meursault's neighbors. Salamano owns an old dog that suffers from mange, and he frequently curses at and beats his pet. However, after Salamano loses his dog, he weeps and longs for its return. His strong grief over losing his dog contrasts with Meursault's indifference at losing his mother.

The Arab The brother of Raymond's mistress. On the Sunday that Raymond, Meursault, and Marie spend at Masson's beach house, Meursault kills the Arab with Raymond's gun. The crime is apparently motiveless—the Arab has done nothing to Meursault. The Arab's mysteriousness as a character makes Meursault's crime all the more strange and difficult to understand.

ANALYSIS OF MAJOR CHARACTERS

MEURSAULT

Meursault is psychologically detached from the world around him. Events that would be very significant for most people, such as a marriage proposal or a parent's death, do not matter to him, at least not on a sentimental level. He simply does not care that his mother is dead, or that Marie loves him.

Meursault is also honest, which means that he does not think of hiding his lack of feeling by shedding false tears over his mother's death. In displaying his indifference, Meursault implicitly challenges society's accepted moral standards, which dictate that one should grieve over death. Because Meursault does not grieve, society sees him as an outsider, a threat, even a monster. At his trial, the fact that he had no reaction to his mother's death damages his reputation far more than his taking of another person's life.

Meursault is neither moral nor immoral. Rather, he is amoral—he simply does not make the distinction between good and bad in his own mind. When Raymond asks him to write a letter that will help Raymond torment his mistress, Meursault indifferently agrees because he "didn't have any reason not to." He does not place any value judgment on his act, and writes the letter mainly because he has the time and the ability to do so.

At the novel's outset, Meursault's indifference seems to apply solely to his understanding of himself. Aside from his atheism, Meursault makes few assumptions about the nature of the world around him. However, his thinking begins to broaden once he is sentenced to death. After his encounter with the chaplain, Meursault concludes that the universe is, like him, totally indifferent to human life. He decides that people's lives have no grand meaning or importance, and that their actions, their comings and goings, have no effect on the world. This realization is the culmination of all the events of the novel. When Meursault accepts "the gentle indifference of the world," he finds peace with himself and with the society around him, and his development as a character is complete.

RAYMOND SINTES

Raymond acts as a catalyst to *The Stranger*'s plot. After Raymond beats and abuses his mistress, he comes into conflict with her brother, an Arab. Raymond draws Meursault into conflict with "the Arab," and eventually Meursault kills the Arab in cold blood. By drawing Meursault into the conflict that eventually results in Meursault's death sentence, Raymond, in a sense, causes Meursault's downfall. This responsibility on Raymond's part is symbolized by the fact that he gives Meursault the gun that Meursault later uses to kill the Arab. However, because the murder and subsequent trial bring about Meursault's realization of the indifference of the universe, Raymond can also be seen as a catalyst of Meursault's "enlightenment."

Because Raymond's character traits contrast greatly with Meursault's, he also functions as a foil for Meursault. Whereas Meursault is simply *amoral*, Raymond is clearly *immoral*. Raymond's treatment of his mistress is violent and cruel, and he nearly kills the Arab himself before Meursault talks him out of it. Additionally, whereas Meursault passively reacts to the events around him, Raymond initiates action. He invites Meursault to dinner and to the beach, and he seeks out the Arabs after his first fight with them.

There is ambiguity in Raymond's relationship with Meursault. On the one hand, Raymond uses Meursault. He easily convinces Meursault to help him in his schemes to punish his mistress, and to testify on his behalf at the police station. On the other hand, Raymond seems to feel some loyalty toward Meursault. He asserts Meursault's innocence at the murder trial, attributing the events leading up to the killing to "chance." It is possible that Raymond begins his relationship with Meursault intending only to use him, and then, like Marie, becomes drawn to Meursault's peculiarities.

MARIE CARDONA

Like Meursault, Marie delights in physical contact. She kisses Meursault frequently in public and enjoys the act of sex. However, unlike Meursault's physical affection for Marie, Marie's physical affection for Meursault signals a deeper sentimental and emotional attachment. Though Marie is disappointed when Meursault expresses his indifference toward love and marriage, she does not end the relationship or rethink her desire to marry him. In fact,

Meursault's strange behavior seems part of his appeal for her. She says that she probably loves him because he is so peculiar. There also may be an element of pragmatism in Marie's decision to marry Meursault. She enjoys a good deal of freedom within the relationship because he does not take any interest in her life when they are not together.

Whatever her motivations for entering into the relationship, Marie remains loyal to Meursault when he is arrested and put on trial. In the context of Camus's absurdist philosophy, Marie's loyalty represents a mixed blessing, because her feelings of faith and hope prevent her from reaching the understanding that Meursault attains at the end of the novel. Marie never grasps the indifference of the universe, and she never comes to understand the redemptive value of abandoning hope. Camus implies that Marie, lacking the deeper understanding of the universe that Meursault has attained, is less "enlightened" than Meursault.

CHARACTER ANALYSIS

THEMES, MOTIFS & SYMBOLS

THEMES

Themes are the fundamental and often universal ideas explored in a literary work.

THE IRRATIONALITY OF THE UNIVERSE

Though *The Stranger* is a work of fiction, it contains a strong resonance of Camus's philosophical notion of absurdity. In his essays, Camus asserts that individual lives and human existence in general have no rational meaning or order. However, because people have difficulty accepting this notion, they constantly attempt to identify or create rational structure and meaning in their lives. The term "absurdity" describes humanity's futile attempt to find rational order where none exists.

Though Camus does not explicitly refer to the notion of absurdity in *The Stranger,* the tenets of absurdity operate within the novel. Neither the external world in which Meursault lives nor the internal world of his thoughts and attitudes possesses any rational order. Meursault has no discernable reason for his actions, such as his decision to marry Marie and his decision to kill the Arab.

Society nonetheless attempts to fabricate or impose rational explanations for Meursault's irrational actions. The idea that things sometimes happen for no reason, and that events sometimes have no meaning is disruptive and threatening to society. The trial sequence in Part Two of the novel represents society's attempt to manufacture rational order. The prosecutor and Meursault's lawyer both offer explanations for Meursault's crime that are based on logic, reason, and the concept of cause and effect. Yet these explanations have no basis in fact and serve only as attempts to defuse the frightening idea that the universe is irrational. The entire trial is therefore an example of absurdity—an instance of humankind's futile attempt to impose rationality on an irrational universe.

The Meaninglessness of Human Life

A second major component of Camus's absurdist philosophy is the idea that human life has no redeeming meaning or purpose. Camus argues that the only certain thing in life is the inevitability of death, and, because all humans will eventually meet death, all lives are all equally meaningless. Meursault gradually moves toward this realization throughout the novel, but he does not fully grasp it until after his argument with the chaplain in the final chapter. Meursault realizes that, just as he is indifferent to much of the universe, so is the universe indifferent to him. Like all people, Meursault has been born, will die, and will have no further importance.

Paradoxically, only after Meursault reaches this seemingly dismal realization is he able to attain happiness. When he fully comes to terms with the inevitability of death, he understands that it does not matter whether he dies by execution or lives to die a natural death at an old age. This understanding enables Meursault to put aside his fantasies of escaping execution by filing a successful legal appeal. He realizes that these illusory hopes, which had previously preoccupied his mind, would do little more than create in him a false sense that death is avoidable. Meursault sees that his hope for sustained life has been a burden. His liberation from this false hope means he is free to live life for what it is, and to make the most of his remaining days.

The Importance of the Physical World

The Stranger shows Meursault to be interested far more in the physical aspects of the world around him than in its social or emotional aspects. This focus on the sensate world results from the novel's assertion that there exists no higher meaning or order to human life. Throughout *The Stranger,* Meursault's attention centers on his own body, on his physical relationship with Marie, on the weather, and on other physical elements of his surroundings. For example, the heat during the funeral procession causes Meursault far more pain than the thought of burying his mother. The sun on the beach torments Meursault, and during his trial Meursault even identifies his suffering under the sun as the reason he killed the Arab. The style of Meursault's narration also reflects his interest in the physical. Though he offers terse, plain descriptions when glossing over emotional or social situations, his descriptions become vivid and ornate when he discusses topics such as nature and the weather.

MOTIFS

Motifs are recurring structures, contrasts, or literary devices that can help to develop and inform the text's major themes.

DECAY AND DEATH

The different characters in *The Stranger* hold widely varying attitudes toward decay and death. Salamano loves his decaying, scab-covered dog and he values its companionship, even though most people find it disgusting. Meursault does not show much emotion in response to his mother's death, but the society in which he lives believes that he should be distraught with grief. Additionally, whereas Meursault is content to believe that physical death represents the complete and final end of life, the chaplain holds fast to the idea of an afterlife.

An essential part of Meursault's character development in the novel is his coming to terms with his own attitudes about death. At the end of the novel, he has finally embraced the idea that death is the one inevitable fact of human life, and is able to accept the reality of his impending execution without despair.

WATCHING AND OBSERVATION

Throughout the novel there are instances of characters watching Meursault, or of his watching them. This motif recalls several components of Camus's absurdist philosophy. The constant watching in *The Stranger* suggests humanity's endless search for purpose, and emphasizes the importance of the tangible, visible details of the physical world in a universe where there is no grander meaning.

When Meursault watches people on the street from his balcony, he does so passively, absorbing details but not judging what he sees. By contrast, the people in the courtroom watch Meursault as part of the process of judgment and condemnation. In the courtroom, we learn that many of Meursault's previous actions were being watched without his—or our—knowledge. The Arabs watch Raymond and his friends with implicit antagonism as they walk to the bus. Raymond's neighbors act as spectators to his dispute with his mistress and the police officer, watching with concern or petty curiosity. At times, watching is a mysterious activity, such as when Meursault watches the woman at Celeste's, and later when she watches him in court. The novel's moments of watching and observation reflect humanity's endless search for meaning, which Camus found absurd.

SYMBOLS

Symbols are objects, characters, figures, or colors used to represent abstract ideas or concepts.

THE COURTROOM

In the courtroom drama that comprises the second half of *The Stranger*, the court symbolizes society as a whole. The law functions as the will of the people, and the jury sits in judgment on behalf of the entire community. In *The Stranger*, Camus strengthens this court-as-society symbolism by having nearly every one of the minor characters from the first half of the novel reappear as a witness in the courtroom. Also, the court's attempts to construct a logical explanation for Meursault's crime symbolize humanity's attempts to find rational explanations for the irrational events of the universe. These attempts, which Camus believed futile, exemplify the absurdity Camus outlined in his philosophy.

THE CRUCIFIX

The crucifix that the examining magistrate waves at Meursault symbolizes Christianity, which stands in opposition to Camus's absurdist world view. Whereas absurdism is based on the idea that human life is irrational and purposeless, Christianity conceives of a rational order for the universe based on God's creation and direction of the world, and it invests human life with higher metaphysical meaning.

The crucifix also symbolizes rational belief structures in general. The chaplain's insistence that Meursault turn to God does not necessarily represent a desire that Meursault accept specifically Christian beliefs so much as a desire that he embrace the principle of a meaningful universe in general. When Meursault defies the magistrate by rejecting Christianity, he implicitly rejects all systems that seek to define a rational order within human existence. This defiance causes Meursault to be branded a threat to social order.

SUMMARY & ANALYSIS

PART ONE: CHAPTER 1

SUMMARY

> *Maman died today. Or yesterday maybe, I don't*
> *know.* (See QUOTATIONS, p. 41)

Meursault, the novel's narrator and protagonist, receives a telegram telling him that his mother has died. She had been living in an old persons' home in Marengo, outside of Algiers. Meursault asks his boss for two days' leave from work to attend the funeral. His boss grudgingly grants the request, and makes Meursault feel almost guilty for asking. Meursault catches the two o'clock bus to Marengo, and sleeps for nearly the entire trip.

When Meursault arrives, he meets with the director of the old persons' home, who assures Meursault that he should not feel bad for having sent his mother there. The director asserts that it was the best decision Meursault could have made, given his modest salary. He tells Meursault that a religious funeral has been planned for his mother, but Meursault knows that his mother never cared about religion. After the brief conversation, the director takes Meursault to the small mortuary where his mother's coffin has been placed.

Alone, Meursault sees that the coffin has already been sealed. The caretaker rushes in and offers to open the casket, but Meursault tells him not to bother. To Meursault's annoyance, the caretaker then stays in the room, chatting idly about his life and about how funeral vigils are shorter in the countryside because bodies decompose more quickly in the heat. Meursault thinks this information is "interesting and [makes] sense."

Meursault spends the night keeping vigil over his mother's body. The caretaker offers him a cup of coffee, and, in turn, Meursault gives the caretaker a cigarette. Meursault finds the atmosphere in the mortuary pleasant and he dozes off. He is awakened by the sound of his mother's friends from the old persons' home shuffling into the mortuary. One of the women cries mournfully, annoying Meursault. Eventually he falls back asleep, as do nearly all of his mother's friends.

The next morning, the day of the funeral, Meursault again meets with the director of the old persons' home. The director asks Meursault if he wants to see his mother one last time before the coffin is sealed permanently, but Meursault declines. The director tells Meursault about Thomas Perez, the only resident of the home who will be allowed to attend the funeral. Perez and Meursault's mother had become nearly inseparable before she died. Other residents had joked that he was her fiancé.

The funeral procession slowly makes its way toward the village. When one of the undertaker's assistants asks Meursault if his mother was old, Meursault responds vaguely because he does not know her exact age. The oppressive heat weighs heavily on him during the long walk. He notices that Thomas Perez cannot keep up, and keeps falling behind the procession. A nurse tells Meursault that he will get sunstroke if he walks too slowly, but will work up a sweat and catch a chill in church if he walks too quickly. Meursault agrees, thinking, "There was no way out." He remembers little of the funeral, aside from Perez's tear-soaked face and the fact that the old man fainted from the heat. As he rides home on the bus to Algiers, Meursault is filled with joy at the prospect of a good night's sleep.

———————————————

ANALYSIS

> *She was right. There was no way out.*
> (See QUOTATIONS, p. 42)

Meursault immediately reveals himself to be indifferent toward emotion and interaction with others. Instead of grieving at the news of his mother's death, he is cold, detached, and indifferent. When he receives the telegram, his primary concern is figuring out on which day his mother died. The fact that he has no emotional reaction at all makes Meursault difficult to categorize. If he were happy that his mother died, he could be cast simply as immoral or a monster. But Meursault is neither happy nor unhappy—he is indifferent.

Though Meursault tends to ignore the emotional, social, and interpersonal content of situations, he is far from indifferent when it comes to the realm of the physical and practical. In this chapter, Meursault focuses on the practical details surrounding his mother's death. He worries about borrowing appropriate funeral clothing from a friend, and he is interested in the caretaker's anecdote about how the length of a vigil depends on how long it takes before the body begins to decompose.

Meursault takes particular interest in nature and the weather. Just before the funeral, he is able to enjoy the beautiful weather and scenery, despite the sad occasion. Similarly, during the funeral procession, Meursault feels no grief or sadness, but he finds the heat of the day nearly unbearable.

Meursault's narration varies in a way that reflects his attitudes toward the world around him. When describing social or emotional situations, his sentences are short, precise, and offer minimal detail. He tells only the essentials of what he sees or does, rarely using metaphors or other rhetorical flourishes. These meager descriptions display Meursault's indifference to society and to the people around him. Meursault's narrative expands greatly when he talks about topics, such as the weather, that directly relate to his physical condition. When describing the effects of the heat during the funeral procession, for instance, he employs metaphor, personification, and other literary devices.

Meursault's belief that the world is meaningless and purposeless becomes apparent in this chapter through Camus's use of irony. Thomas Perez, the one person who actually cares about Madame Meursault, cannot keep up with her funeral procession because of his ailing physical condition. This sad detail is incompatible with any sentimental or humanistic interpretation of Madame Meursault's death. Perez's slowness is simply the result of his old age, and no grand or comforting meaning can be assigned to it or drawn from it. We frequently see such irony undercutting any notions of a higher, controlling order operating within *The Stranger*.

PART ONE: CHAPTERS 2–3

SUMMARY: CHAPTER 2

Meursault suddenly realizes why his boss was annoyed at his request for two days' leave from work. Because his mother's funeral was on a Friday, counting the weekend, Meursault essentially received four days off rather than two. Meursault goes swimming at a public beach, where he runs into Marie Cardona, a former coworker of his. He helps her onto a float, and after admiring her beauty, he climbs up next to her on the float. He rests his head on her body, and they lie together for a while, looking at the sky. They swim happily together and flirt over the course of the afternoon, and Marie accepts Meursault's invitation to see a movie. She is somewhat surprised to learn that Meursault's mother was buried just a day earlier, but she quickly forgets it. After the movie, Marie spends the night with Meursault.

Marie is gone when Meursault awakes. He decides against having his usual lunch at Celeste's because he wants to avoid the inevitable questions about his mother. He stays in bed until noon, then spends the entire afternoon on his balcony, smoking, eating, and observing the assorted people on the street as they come and go. The weather is beautiful. As evening approaches, Meursault buys some food and cooks dinner. After his meal he muses that yet another Sunday is over. His mother is buried, and he must return to work in the morning. He concludes that nothing has changed after all.

SUMMARY: CHAPTER 3

The next day, Meursault goes to work. His boss is friendly and asks Meursault about his mother. Meursault and his co-worker, Emmanuel, go to Celeste's for lunch. Celeste asks Meursault if everything is alright, but Meursault changes the subject after only a brief response. He takes a nap and then returns to work for the rest of the afternoon. After work, Meursault runs into his neighbor, Salamano, who is on the stairs with his dog. The dog suffers from mange, so its skin has the same scabby appearance as its elderly master's. Salamano walks the dog twice a day, beating it and swearing at it all the while.

Raymond Sintes, another neighbor, invites Meursault to dinner. Raymond is widely believed to be a pimp, but when anyone asks about his occupation he replies that he is a "warehouse guard." Over dinner, Raymond requests Meursault's advice about something, and then asks Meursault whether he would like to be "pals." Meursault offers no objection, so Raymond launches into his story.

Raymond tells Meursault that when he suspected that his mistress was cheating on him, he beat her, and she left him. This altercation led Raymond into a fight with his mistress's brother, an Arab. Raymond is still attracted to his mistress, but wants to punish her for her infidelity. His idea is to write a letter to incite her guilt and make her return to him. He plans to sleep with her, and "right at the last minute," spit in her face. Raymond then asks Meursault to write the letter, and Meursault responds that he would not mind doing it. Raymond is pleased with Meursault's effort, so he tells Meursault that they are now "pals." In his narrative, Meursault reflects that he "didn't mind" being pals with Raymond. As Meursault returns to his room, he hears Salamano's dog crying softly.

ANALYSIS: CHAPTERS 2–3

Meursault appears heartless for failing to express grief or even to care about his mother's death. Yet to condemn and dismiss him risks missing much of the meaning of the novel. *The Stranger,* though it explores Camus's philosophy of the absurd, is not meant to be read as a tale containing a lesson for our moral improvement. Camus's philosophy of the absurd characterizes the world and human existence as having no rational purpose or meaning. According to Camus's philosophy, the universe is indifferent to human struggles, and Meursault's indifferent personality embodies this philosophy. He does not attempt to assign a rational order to the events around him, and he is largely indifferent to human activity. Because Meursault does not see his mother's death as part of a larger structure of human existence, he can easily make a date, go to a comedy, and have sex the day after his mother's funeral. Meursault is Camus's example of someone who does not need a rational world view to function.

Meursault's interactions with Marie on the beach show the importance he places on the physical aspects of existence. He reports to us almost nothing about Marie's personality, but he carefully describes their physical interactions. The prose in his description of lying on the float with Marie and looking up at the sky is unusually warm and heartfelt. In this passage, it even seems that Meursault is happy. When he describes watching people from his balcony the following day, he again seems content.

While watching from his balcony, Meursault does not express any sort of judgment about the people he sees—he simply notices their primary characteristics. While the people he watches obviously attach great importance to their own activities, Meursault sees them as just part of another Sunday, like any other. Throughout the novel, Meursault plays this role of the detached observer. Just as he does not pass judgment on those he sees from far above on his balcony, so too does he refrain from judging the more significant characters with whom he interacts throughout the novel. Meursault will not commit to either condemning or defending Salamano's treatment of his dog. Likewise, while he does not expressly condone Raymond's treatment of his mistress, neither does Meursault refuse to participate in Raymond's scheme.

Meursault and Raymond seem to display similarly indifferent responses to the world around them, but Raymond in fact serves as a foil for Meursault. In contrast with Meursault, who is amoral, meaning he does not make moral distinctions, Raymond is clearly *immoral*: he beats up his mistress and he fights with her brother. Moreover, Raymond's manner of convincing Meursault to assist him in his scheme to take further revenge on his mistress seems somewhat manipulative. Raymond's plan for revenge crystallizes the distinction between Meursault and Raymond. Raymond plans to make love to his mistress and then spit in her face. He uses the physical act of sex as a tool for humiliation and revenge. Meursault, conversely, sees his sexual affair with Marie as a source of delight, in much the same way that he responds positively to other physical aspects of life.

PART ONE: CHAPTERS 4–5

SUMMARY: CHAPTER 4

[S]he asked me if I loved her. I told her it didn't mean anything but that I didn't think so.
(See QUOTATIONS, p. 43)

The following Saturday, Meursault goes swimming again with Marie. He is intensely aroused from the first moment he sees her. After the swim, they hurry back to Meursault's apartment to have sex. Marie spends the night and stays for lunch the following day. Meursault tells her the story of Salamano and his dog, and she laughs. Then Marie asks Meursault if he loves her. He replies that, though "it [doesn't] mean anything, he [doesn't] think so." Meursault's response makes Marie look sad.

Marie and Meursault can hear an argument in Raymond's apartment. The tenants of the building gather on the landing and listen outside the door to the sounds of Raymond beating his mistress. A police officer arrives. Raymond's mistress informs the officer that Raymond beat her and the cop slaps Raymond in the face. He then orders Raymond to wait in his apartment until he is summoned to the police station. Later that afternoon, Raymond visits Meursault in his apartment. He asks Meursault to go to the police station to testify that his mistress had cheated on him. Meursault agrees. After an evening out, the two men return to their apartment building to find Salamano desperately searching for his dog, who ran away from him at the Parade Ground. Meursault says that if the dog is at the pound, he can pay a fee to have it returned. Salamano curses the dog when he hears this, but later that night, Meursault hears Salamano crying in his room.

SUMMARY: CHAPTER 5

> *I said that people never change their lives, that in any case one life was as good as another and that I wasn't dissatisfied with mine here at all.*
>
> (See QUOTATIONS, p. 44)

Raymond's friend Masson invites Meursault and Marie to spend the following Sunday at his beach house with him, his wife, and Raymond. Meursault's boss offers him a position in a new office he plans to open in Paris. Meursault replies that it is all the same to him, and his boss becomes angry at his lack of ambition. Meursault muses that he used to have ambition as a student, but then realized that none of it really mattered.

Marie asks Meursault if he wants to marry her. Meursault replies that it makes no difference to him. When she asks Meursault if he loves her, he again replies that though it does not mean anything, he probably does not love her. Marie thinks he is peculiar, but decides that she wants to marry him nonetheless. She tells Meursault that she cannot have dinner with him that night, and when he does not ask why she laughs. Meursault eats dinner alone at Celeste's, where he notices a strange woman obsessively checking off radio programs listed in a magazine. He follows her briefly when she leaves.

Meursault returns home and finds Salamano waiting outside his door. Salamano says that he bought his dog in an effort to overcome the loneliness he felt after his wife died, and that he does not want to get a new dog because he is used to the old one. Salamano then expresses his condolences for the death of Madame Meursault. He mentions that some people in the neighborhood thought badly of Meursault for sending her to the home, but he himself knew that Meursault must have loved her very much. He returns to his own loss, saying that he does not know what he will do without his dog. Its loss has changed his life dramatically.

ANALYSIS: CHAPTERS 4–5

On the surface, Meursault appears to be an ordinary, lower middle-class French colonial in Algeria, living a typical day-to-day routine. He eats lunch in small cafés, attends films, and swims during his free time. He is diligent but not exceptional at his perfectly ordinary job. As of yet, he challenges nothing this society hands him, and it challenges nothing in him. Meursault lives his life almost unconsciously, nearly sleepwalking through a ready-made structure that his society provides him.

By attempting to assign meaning to the meaningless events of Meursault's life, the people in Meursault's social circle succumb to the same temptation that confronts us as we read *The Stranger*. Salamano, for example, states that he is sure that Meursault loved his mother deeply, despite the fact that Meursault offers no evidence to support such an assertion. Salamano is himself supplying the rational order that he desires to find in the world. His statement about Meursault's love for his mother seems intended to comfort himself more than to comfort Meursault. Further, the way Salamano turns to the subject of Meursault's love for his mother in the midst of his own discussion of his missing dog suggests that Salamano uses his discussion of Meursault and Madame Meursault to displace his own guilt. Salamano assumes that Meursault really loved his mother despite sending her to a nursing home, just as he loved his dog even though he beat it.

Raymond's encounter with the policeman implies a lack of rational order in human life. Society deems Raymond's slapping of his mistress for a perceived injustice an immoral act. But when the cop slaps Raymond, society in effect condones slapping. Physically, both slaps are nearly identical, yet one is considered wrong, and the other, just and good. Through the policeman's actions, Camus implicitly challenges the truth of society's accepted moral order.

Salamano's description of life with his dog highlights the inevitability of physical decay. Salamano says that he initially had human companionship in his wife, but she died and he had to settle for the animal companionship of his dog. As time has passed, Salamano's dog has become increasingly ugly and sick, until the point where it, too, has left him. Physical decay represents a marker and reminder of Camus's philosophy of the absurd, which asserts that humans are thrust into a life that inevitably ends in death.

Meursault narrates the events of his life as they occur without interpreting them as a coherent narrative. He does not relate the events of earlier chapters to the events that take place in these chapters. It becomes clear that Meursault concentrates largely on the moment in which he finds himself, with little reference to past occurrences or future consequences. This outlook perhaps explains his ambivalent attitude toward marriage with Marie. Because he does not think about what married life would be like, Meursault does not particularly care whether or not he and Marie marry. Characteristically, the emotional and sentimental aspects of marriage never enter into his mind.

PART ONE: CHAPTER 6

SUMMARY

The following Sunday, Meursault has difficulty waking up. Marie has to shake him and shout at him. He finally awakens and the two go downstairs. On the way down they call Raymond out of his room, and the three of them prepare to take a bus to Masson's beach house. As they head for the bus, they notice a group of Arabs, including Raymond's mistress's brother—whom Meursault refers to as "the Arab"—staring at them. Raymond is relieved when the Arabs do not board the bus. As the bus leaves, Meursault looks back and sees that the Arabs are still staring blankly at the same spot.

Masson's beach house is a small wooden bungalow. Meursault meets Masson's wife, and for the first time thinks about what marrying Marie will be like. Masson, Meursault, and Marie swim until lunchtime. Marie and Meursault swim in tandem, enjoying themselves greatly. After lunch, Masson, Raymond, and Meursault take a walk while the two women clean the dishes. The heat on the beach is nearly unbearable for Meursault. The three men notice two Arabs, one of whom is the brother of Raymond's mistress, following them. A fight quickly breaks out. Raymond and Masson have the advantage until Raymond's adversary produces a knife. Meursault tries to warn Raymond, but it is too late. The Arab slashes Raymond's arm and mouth before retreating with his friend. Masson and Meursault help the wounded Raymond back to the bungalow. Marie looks very frightened, and Madame Masson cries when she sees Raymond's injuries. Masson takes Raymond to a nearby doctor. Meursault does not feel like explaining what happened, so he smokes cigarettes and watches the sea.

Raymond returns to the bungalow later that afternoon, wrapped in bandages. He descends to the beach, and, against Raymond's wishes, Meursault follows along. Raymond finds the two Arabs lying down beside a spring. Raymond has a gun in his pocket, which he fingers nervously as the two Arabs stare at him. Meursault tries to convince Raymond not to shoot, and eventually talks him into handing over the gun. The Arabs then sneak away behind a rock, so Meursault and Raymond leave.

Meursault accompanies Raymond back to the beach house. The intense heat has worn Meursault out, so the prospect of walking up the stairs to face the women seems just as tiring as continuing to walk on the hot beach. Meursault chooses to stay on the beach. The heat is oppressive and Meursault has a headache, so he walks back to the spring to cool off. When Meursault reaches the spring, he sees that the brother of Raymond's mistress has returned as well. Meursault puts his hand on the gun. When Meursault steps toward the cool water of the spring, the Arab draws his knife. The sunlight reflects off the blade and directly into Meursault's eyes, which are already stinging with sweat and heat. Meursault fires the gun once. He pauses and then fires four more times into the Arab's motionless body. Meursault has killed the Arab.

ANALYSIS: CHAPTER 6

At the beginning of the novel, the indifference Meursault feels is located exclusively within himself, in his own heart and mind. By this point, however, Meursault has come to realize how similar the universe—or at least Camus's conception of it—is to his own personality. He begins to understand that not only does *he* not care what happens, but that *the world* does not care either. Reflecting on the moment when Raymond gave him the gun, Meursault says, "It was then that I realized you could either shoot or not shoot." His comment implies that no difference exists between the two alternatives.

This chapter represents the climax of the first part of the book. Since his return from his mother's funeral, everything that Meursault has done in the narrative up to this point—meeting Marie, meeting Raymond, and becoming involved in the affair with Raymond's mistress—has led him to the beach house. Yet Meursault's murder of the Arab comes as a complete surprise—nothing in *The Stranger* has prepared us for it. The feeling of abruptness that accompanies this shift in the plot is intentional on Camus's part. He wants the murder to happen unexpectedly and to strike us as bizarre.

Inevitably, the first question that the killing provokes is, "Why?" But nothing in Meursault's narrative answers this question. Camus's philosophy of absurdism emphasizes the futility of man's inevitable attempts to find order and meaning in life. The "absurd" refers to the feeling man experiences when he tries to find or fabricate order in an irrational universe. Cleverly, Camus coaxes us into just such an attempt—he lures us into trying to determine the reason for Meursault's killing of the Arab, when in fact Meursault has no reason. Camus forces us to confront the fact that any rational explanation we try to offer would be based on a consciousness that *we* create for Meursault, an order that *we* impose onto his mind.

In this chapter, we once again see the profound effect nature has on Meursault. Early in the chapter, Meursault notes nature's benefits. The sun soothes his headache, and the cool water provides an opportunity for him and Marie to swim and play happily together. Later in the chapter, however, nature becomes a negative force on Meursault. As at his mother's funeral, the heat oppresses him. Camus's language intensifies to describe the sun's harshness, particularly in the passages just before Meursault commits the murder. His prose becomes increasingly ornate, featuring such rhetorical devices as personification and metaphor, and contrasting strongly with the spare, simple descriptions that Meursault usually offers.

PART TWO: CHAPTERS 1–2

SUMMARY: CHAPTER 1

Meursault has been arrested and thrown into jail for murdering the Arab. Meursault's young, court-appointed lawyer visits him in his cell and informs him that investigators have checked into Meursault's private life and learned that he "show[ed] insensitivity" on the day of Madame Meursault's funeral. The lawyer asks if Meursault was sad at his mother's burial, and Meursault responds that he does not usually analyze himself. He says that though he probably did love his mother, "that didn't mean anything." The lawyer departs, disgusted by Meursault's indifference to his mother's death. Meursault says, "I felt the urge to reassure [the lawyer] that I was . . . just like everybody else."

That afternoon, Meursault is taken to meet with the examining magistrate. The magistrate asks Meursault whether he loved his mother, and Meursault replies that he loved her as much as anyone. The magistrate asks why Meursault paused between the first shot at the Arab and other four shots. Nothing about the crime bothers the magistrate aside from this detail. When Meursault does not answer, the magistrate waves a crucifix at him and asks if he believes in God. Meursault says no. The magistrate states that his own life would be meaningless if he doubted the existence of God, and concludes that Meursault has an irrevocably hardened soul. During the course of the eleven-month investigation that ensues, the magistrate takes to calling Meursault "Monsieur Antichrist," with an almost cordial air.

SUMMARY: CHAPTER 2

Meursault describes his first few days in prison. The authorities initially put him in a cell with a number of other people, including several Arabs. Eventually, Meursault is taken to a private cell. One day, Marie comes to visit him. The visiting room is noisy and crowded with prisoners and their visitors. Marie wears a forced smile, and tells Meursault that he needs to have hope. She says she believes that he will be acquitted, and that they will get married and go swimming. Meursault, however, seems more interested in the mournful prisoner sitting beside him, whose mother is visiting. Marie leaves, and later sends a letter stating that the authorities will not allow her to visit Meursault anymore because she is not his wife.

Meursault's desires to go swimming, to smoke cigarettes, and to have sex torment him in jail. He becomes accustomed to his confinement, however, so it ceases to be a terrible punishment. Only the early evenings seem to trouble him. He sleeps as many hours as possible, and kills time by recalling the tiniest details of his apartment and thinking about a story on an old scrap of newspaper he has found in his cell. The story involves a Czechoslovakian man who left his village at a young age. After making his fortune, he returned to his village in disguise to see his mother and sister, who were running a hotel. He planned to surprise them by revealing his identity after showing off his wealth. Unfortunately, his mother and sister killed him and robbed him before he could reveal himself. When they discovered their mistake, the two women both committed suicide.

Analysis: Chapters 1–2

The magistrate, when he waves a crucifix at Meursault, introduces the notion that Meursault and his attitudes represent a threat to society. Meursault's atheism and indifference to his mother's death implicitly challenge the magistrate's belief in a rational universe controlled by God—the belief that gives his life meaning. By associating Meursault with the devil and calling him "Monsieur Antichrist," the magistrate attempts to categorize Meursault in terms of Christianity, the magistrate's own belief system. The magistrate incorporates Meursault into his ordered world view and then dismisses him as evil, thereby preventing Meursault from undermining his rational structure of belief.

For the most part, Meursault reacts to his confinement in prison with characteristic indifference. Most important, his imprisonment does not incite any guilt or regret over what he has done. As at his mother's funeral, Meursault focuses on the practical details of his life in prison rather than on its emotional elements. For instance, he thinks the fact that the court will appoint an attorney for him is "very convenient." He also enjoys the examining magistrate's friendly demeanor in their subsequent meetings, and does not treat him as an adversary. Not surprisingly, the physical aspects of confinement weigh most heavily on Meursault's mind. His unsatisfied longings for nature, the ocean, cigarettes, and sex constitute, in his mind, his punishment. He notes that though he thinks about women, he does not think about Marie in particular. This statement underscores the physical, nonemotional character of their relationship.

At the end of Part Two, Chapter 2, Meursault, staring at his reflection in the window, notes the seriousness of his face and suddenly realizes that he has been talking to himself. Meursault's actions signal his emerging self-awareness and self-consciousness. In prison, he is growing to understand himself and his beliefs more and more. He decides that he could get used to any living situation, even living in a tree trunk, for example.

Most important, Meursault begins to gain insight into the irrational universe around him. In his mind echo the words of the nurse who speaks to him in Part One, Chapter 1, during the funeral procession. She told Meursault that he would get sunstroke if he walked too slowly, but would work up a sweat and catch a chill in church if he walked too quickly. At the time, Meursault agreed that "there was no way out," but now he understands for the first time the full implications of these words: there is no way out of prison, and there is no way out of a life that inevitably and purposelessly ends in death. When Marie comes to visit Meursault, her hope that Meursault's trial will end happily contrasts strongly with Meursault's growing affirmation of an irrational universe.

The news article that Meursault studies about the Czechoslovakian man serves to comment and expand upon the themes of absurdism that Camus illustrates in *The Stranger*. Camus's absurdist philosophy asserts that the events of the world have no rational order or discernible meaning. The story of the returning son murdered by his mother and sister fits perfectly into such a belief system. There is no reason for the son to have died. His terrible, ironic fate is not compatible with any logical or ordered system governing human existence. Like Meursault's killing of the Arab, the son's death is a purposeless, meaningless tragedy that defies rationalization or justification.

PART TWO: CHAPTERS 3–4

SUMMARY: CHAPTER 3

The following summer, Meursault's trial begins. Meursault is surprised to find the courtroom packed with people. Even the woman he saw checking off radio programs at Celeste's is there. The press has given his case a great deal of publicity because the summer is a slow season for news.

The judge asks Meursault why he put his mother in a home. Meursault replies that he did not have enough money to care for her. When the judge asks Meursault if the decision tormented him, Meursault explains that both he and his mother became used to their new situations because they did not expect anything from one another.

The director of the home confirms that Madame Meursault complained about Meursault's decision to put her in the home. The director says that he was surprised by Meursault's "calm" during his mother's funeral. He remembers that Meursault declined to see his mother's body and did not cry once. One of the undertaker's assistants reported that Meursault did not even know how old his mother was. Meursault realizes that the people in the courtroom hate him.

The caretaker testifies that Meursault smoked a cigarette and drank coffee during his vigil. Meursault's lawyer insists the jury take note that the caretaker had likewise smoked during the vigil, accepting Meursault's offer of a cigarette. After the caretaker admits to offering Meursault coffee in the first place, the prosecutor derides Meursault as a disloyal son for not refusing the coffee. Thomas Perez takes the stand and recalls being too overcome with sadness during the funeral to notice whether or not Meursault cried. Celeste, claiming Meursault as his friend, attributes Meursault's killing of the Arab to bad luck. Marie's testimony reveals Meursault's plan to marry her. The prosecutor stresses that Marie and Meursault's sexual relationship began the weekend after the funeral and that they went to see a comedy at the movie theater that day. Favorable accounts—of Meursault's honesty and decency from Masson, and of Meursault's kindness to Salamano's dog from Salamano—counter the prosecutor's accusations. Raymond testifies that it was just by chance that Meursault became involved in his dispute with his mistress's brother. The prosecutor retorts by asking if it was just chance that Meursault wrote the letter to Raymond's mistress, testified on Raymond's behalf at the police station, and went to the beach the day of the crime.

Summary: Chapter 4

In his closing argument, the prosecutor cites Meursault's obvious intelligence and lack of remorse as evidence of premeditated murder. Reminding the jury that the next trial on the court's schedule involves parricide (the murder of a close relative), the prosecutor alleges that Meursault's lack of grief over his mother's death threatens the moral basis of society. In a moral sense, the prosecutor argues, Meursault is just as guilty as the man who killed his own father. Calling for the death penalty, the prosecutor elaborates that Meursault's actions have paved the way for the man who killed his father, so Meursault must be considered guilty of the other man's crime as well.

Meursault denies having returned to the beach with the intention of killing the Arab. When the judge asks him to clarify his motivation for the crime, Meursault blurts out that he did it "because of the sun." Meursault's lawyer claims that Meursault did a noble thing by sending his mother to a home because he could not afford to care for her. Making Meursault feel further excluded from his own case, Meursault's lawyer offers an interpretation of the events that led up to the crime, speaking in the first person, as though he were Meursault. Meursault's mind drifts again during his lawyer's interminable argument. Meursault is found guilty of premeditated murder and sentenced to death by guillotine.

ANALYSIS: CHAPTERS 3–4

In *The Stranger,* Camus seeks to undermine the sense of reassurance that courtroom dramas typically provide. Such narratives reassure us not only that truth will always prevail, but that truth actually exists. They uphold our judicial system as just, despite its flaws. Ultimately, these narratives reassure us that we live in a world governed by reason and order. Camus sees such reassurance as a silly and false illusion. Because there is no rational explanation for Meursault's murder of the Arab, the authorities seek to construct an explanation of their own, which they base on false assumptions. By imposing a rational order on logically unrelated events, the authorities make Meursault appear to be a worse character than he is.

Camus portrays the process of accusation and judgment as hopeless, false, and irrational. Society demands that a rational interpretation be imposed on the facts and events of Meursault's life, whether or not such an interpretation is possible. Meursault's lawyer and the prosecutor both offer false explanations, leaving the jury with a choice between two lies. The prosecutor manufactures a meaningful, rational connection between Meursault's trial and the upcoming parricide trial, even though no actual link exists between the two cases. However, the prosecutor has no trouble imposing enough meaning to convince the jury that a link *does* in fact exist, and that Meursault deserves a death sentence.

During his trial, Meursault comes to understand that his failure to interpret or find meaning in his own life has left him vulnerable to others, who will impose such meaning for him. Until this point, Meursault has unthinkingly drifted from moment to moment, lacking the motivation or ability to examine his life as a narrative with a past, present, and future. Even during the early part of trial he watches as if everything were happening to someone else. Only well into the trial does Meursault suddenly realize that the prosecutor has successfully manufactured an interpretation of Meursault's life, and that, in the jury's eyes, he likely appears guilty. Meursault's own lawyer not only imposes yet another manufactured interpretation of Meursault's life, but even goes so far as to deliver this interpretation in the first person, effectively stealing Meursault's own point of view when making the argument.

The trial forces Meursault to confront his existence consciously because he is suddenly being held accountable for it. As he hears positive, negative, and neutral interpretations of his character, he recognizes that part of his being evades his control, because it exists only in the minds of others. All the witnesses discuss the same man, Meursault, but they offer differing interpretations of his character. In each testimony, meaning is constructed exclusively by the witness—Meursault has nothing to do with it.

PART TWO: CHAPTER 5

SUMMARY

> [F]or the first time, in that night alive with signs and stars, I opened myself to the gentle indifference of the world.... For everything to be consummated, for me to feel less alone, I had only to wish that there be a large crowd of spectators the day of my execution and that they greet me with cries of hate.
>
> (See QUOTATIONS, p. 45)

After his trial, Meursault only cares about escaping the "machinery of justice" that has condemned him to death. The newspapers characterize the situation of a condemned man in terms of a "debt owed to society," but Meursault believes the only thing that matters is the possibility of an escape to freedom. He remembers his mother telling him how his father once forced himself to watch an execution. Afterward, Meursault's father vomited several times. Now, Meursault thinks an execution is really the only thing of interest for a man. He only wishes he could be a spectator instead of the victim. He fantasizes about a combination of chemicals that would kill the condemned only nine times out of ten, because then at least he would have a chance of surviving.

Meursault also dislikes the fact that the guillotine forces the condemned to hope that the execution works on the first try. If the first attempt fails, the execution will be painful. Hence, the prisoner is forced into "moral collaboration" with the execution process, by hoping for its success. He further objects to the fact that the guillotine is mounted on the ground, not on a scaffold. The condemned is killed "with a little shame and with great precision." Meursault counts himself lucky every time dawn passes without the sound of footsteps approaching his cell, because he knows that such footsteps would signal the arrival of the men who will take him to his execution. When he considers the option of filing a legal appeal, Meursault initially assumes the worst, believing any appeal would be denied.

Only after considering the fact that everyone dies eventually does he allow himself to consider the possibility of a pardon and freedom. Whenever he thinks of this possibility, he feels delirious joy.

Against Meursault's wishes, the chaplain visits and asks why Meursault has refused to see him. Meursault reasserts his denial of God's existence. When the chaplain states that Meursault's attitude results from "extreme despair," Meursault says he is afraid, not desperate. The chaplain insists that all the condemned men he has known have eventually turned to God for comfort. Meursault becomes irritated by the chaplain's insistence that he spend the rest of his life thinking about God. He feels he has no time to waste with God. The chaplain tells Meursault that his "heart is blind."

Meursault suddenly becomes enraged. He shouts that nothing matters, and that nothing in the chaplain's beliefs is as certain as the chaplain thinks. The only certainty Meursault perceives in the whole of human existence is death. In the course of his outburst, Meursault grabs the chaplain. After the guards separate them, Meursault realizes why his mother started her little romance with Thomas Perez. She lived in the midst of fading lives, so she chose to play at living life over again. He believes crying over her would simply be an insult to her. Meursault has finally shed any glimmer of hope, so he opens himself to the "gentle indifference of the world." His only hope is that there will be a crowd of angry spectators at his execution who will greet him "with cries of hate."

ANALYSIS

While awaiting his execution, Meursault takes the final step in the development of his consciousness. Whereas during his trial Meursault passively observed the judgments leveled against him, in prison he begins to ponder the fact of his inevitable death. He begins to see his life as having a past, present, and future, and concludes that there is no difference between dying soon by execution and dying decades later of natural causes. This capacity for self-analysis is a new development for Meursault, and it contrasts greatly with his level of self-awareness earlier in the novel.

Once Meursault dismisses his perceived difference between execution and natural death, he must deal with the concept of hope. Hope only tortures him, because it creates the false illusion that he can change the fact of his death. The leap of hope he feels at the idea of having another twenty years of life prevents him from making the most of his final days or hours. Hope disturbs his calm and understanding, and prevents him from fully coming to grips with his situation.

After speaking with the chaplain, Meursault no longer views his impending execution with hope or despair. He accepts death as an inevitable fact and looks forward to it with peace. This realization of death's inevitability constitutes Meursault's triumph over society. Expressing remorse over his crime would implicitly acknowledge the murder as wrong, and Meursault's punishment as justified. However, Meursault's lack of concern about his death sentence implies that his trial and conviction were pointless exercises. Moreover, Meursault accepts that his views make him an enemy and stranger to society. Meursault anticipates that his position in relation to society will be affirmed when crowds cheer hatefully at him as he is beheaded. Meursault's eager anticipation of this moment shows he is content being an outsider.

In his heightened state of consciousness prior to his execution, Meursault says that he comes to recognize the "gentle indifference of the world." Meursault decides that, like him, the world does not pass judgment, nor does it rationally order or control the events of human existence. Yet Meursault does not despair at this fact. Instead, he draws from it a kind of freedom. Without the need for false hope or illusions of order and meaning, Meursault feels free to live a simpler, less burdened life.

SUMMARY & ANALYSIS

Important Quotations Explained

1. Maman died today. Or yesterday maybe, I don't
   know. I got a telegram from the home: "Mother
   deceased. Funeral tomorrow. Faithfully yours." That
   doesn't mean anything. Maybe it was yesterday.

Spoken by Meursault, the novel's narrator and protagonist, these
are the opening lines of the novel. They introduce Meursault's emotional indifference, one his most important character traits. Meursault does not express any remorse upon learning of his mother's death—he merely reports the fact in a plain and straightforward manner. His chief concern is the precise day of his mother's death—a seemingly trivial detail.

Mersault's comment, "That doesn't mean anything," has at least two possible meanings. It could be taken as part of his discussion about which day Madame Meursault died. That is, Meursault could mean that the telegram does not reveal any meaningful information about the date of his mother's death. However, the comment could also be read more broadly, with a significance that perhaps Meursault does not consciously intend; Meursault might be implying that it does not matter that his mother died at all. This possible reading introduces the idea of the meaninglessness of human existence, a theme that resounds throughout the novel.

2.   She said, "If you go slowly, you risk getting sunstroke.
      But if you go too fast, you work up a sweat and then
      catch a chill inside the church." She was right. There
      was no way out.

The nurse speaks these words to Meursault during the long, hot
funeral procession in Part One, Chapter 1. On a literal level, the
nurse's words describe the dilemma the weather presents: the heat's
influence is inescapable. But Meursault's comment, "There was no
way out," broadens the implications of the nurse's words. As Meursault eventually realizes, the nurse's words describe the human condition: man is born into a life that can only end in death. Death, like
the harsh effects of the sun, is unavoidable. This idea is central to
Camus's philosophy in *The Stranger,* which posits death as the one
central, inescapable fact of life.

3. A minute later she asked me if I loved her. I told her it
    didn't mean anything but that I didn't think so.

In this passage from Part One, Chapter 4, Meursault relates an
exchange he has with Marie. With characteristic emotional indifference and detachment, Meursault answers Marie's question com-
pletely and honestly. Always blunt, he never alters what he says to
be tactful or to conform to societal expectations. However, Meursault's honesty reflects his ignorance. His blunt words suggest that
he does not understand fully the emotional stakes in Marie's question. Also, in Meursault's assertion that love "didn't mean anything," we see an early form of a central idea Meursault later comes
to understand—the meaninglessness of human life.

4.   I said that people never change their lives, that in any
      case one life was as good as another and that I wasn't
      dissatisfied with mine here at all.

This quotation is Meursault's response in Part One, Chapter 5, to his boss's offer of a position in Paris. Meursault's statement shows his belief in a certain rigidity or inertia to human existence. His comment that "one life was as good as another" maintains that although details may change, one's life remains essentially constant. The comment also implies that each person's life is essentially equal to everyone else's.

At this point in the novel, Meursault offers no explanation for his belief in the equality of human lives. In the novel's final chapter, he identifies death as the force responsible for the constant and unchangeable nature of human life. A comparison of this quotation to Meursault's ideas following his death sentence highlights Meursault's development as a character whose understanding of the human condition deepens as a result of his experiences.

5. As if that blind rage had washed me clean, rid me of hope; for the first time, in that night alive with signs and stars, I opened myself to the gentle indifference of the world. Finding it so much like myself—so like a brother, really—I felt that I had been happy and that I was happy again. For everything to be consummated, for me to feel less alone, I had only to wish that there be a large crowd of spectators the day of my execution and that they greet me with cries of hate.

These are the last lines of the novel. After his meeting with the chaplain, whose insistence that Meursault turn to God in the wake of his death sentence puts Meursault into a "blind rage," Meursault fully accepts the absurdist idea that the universe is indifferent to human affairs and that life lacks rational order and meaning. He moves toward this revelation through the course of the novel, but does not fully grasp it until he accepts the impossibility of avoiding his death. Meursault realizes that the universe's indifference to human affairs echoes his own personal indifference to human affairs, and the similarity evokes a feeling of companionship in him that leads him to label the world "a brother."

As opposed to earlier in the novel, when Meursault was passively content at best, here Meursault finds that he is actively happy once he opens himself to the reality of human existence. Meursault finds that he is also happy with his position in society. He does not mind being a loathed criminal. He only wishes for companionship, "to feel less alone." He accepts that this companionship will take the form of an angry mob on his execution day. He sees his impending execution as the "consummation" of his new understanding.

QUOTATIONS

KEY FACTS

FULL TITLE
The Stranger or *L'étranger*

AUTHOR
Albert Camus

TYPE OF WORK
Novel

GENRE
Existential novel; crime drama

LANGUAGE
French

TIME AND PLACE WRITTEN
Early 1940s, France

DATE OF FIRST PUBLICATION
1942

PUBLISHER
Librairie Gallimard, France

NARRATOR
In Part One, Meursault narrates the events of the story almost as they happen. In Part Two, he narrates the events of his trial from jail, then moves into a more immediate narration in Chapter 5.

POINT OF VIEW
Meursault narrates in the first person and limits his account to his own thoughts and perceptions. His description of the other characters is entirely subjective—that is, he does not attempt to portray them in a neutral light or to understand their thoughts and feelings.

TONE
Detached, sober, plain, at times subtly ironic

TENSE
Shifts between immediate past (or real-time narration) and more distant past, with occasional instances where Meursault speaks in the present tense.

SETTING (TIME)
Slightly before World War II

SETTING (PLACE)
Algeria

PROTAGONIST
Meursault

MAJOR CONFLICT
After committing murder, Meursault struggles against society's attempts to manufacture and impose rational explanations for his attitudes and actions. This struggle is embodied by Meursault's battle with the legal system that prosecutes him.

RISING ACTION
Meursault relationship with Marie, his involvement in Raymond's affairs, his trip to Masson's beach house, and his taking of Raymond's gun are the choices Meursault makes that lead up to his killing of the Arab.

CLIMAX
Meursault shoots a man, known as "the Arab," for no apparent reason.

FALLING ACTION
Meursault is arrested for murder, jailed, tried in court, and sentenced to death. He then has an epiphany about "the gentle indifference of the world" after arguing with the chaplain about God's existence.

THEMES
The irrationality of the universe; the meaninglessness of human life; the importance of the physical world

MOTIFS
Decay and death; watching and observation

SYMBOLS
The courtroom; the crucifix

FORESHADOWING
Madame Meursault's friends watching Meursault foreshadows the jury's watching him in judgment.

KEY FACTS

STUDY QUESTIONS &
ESSAY TOPICS

STUDY QUESTIONS

1.   *How do we know the world of* The Stranger *is irrational?
     How do different characters react to this irrationality?*

Camus demonstrates that the world of *The Stranger* is irrational by
excluding from the text any logical explanation for the events of the
novel. Meursault's murder of the Arab is the most obvious example
of an event that occurs for no apparent reason. Meursault has no
reason to kill the Arab, nor does he construct one. His action is com-
pletely random and purposeless. Another occurrence that holds no
rational meaning is Thomas Perez's exhaustion at the funeral. Perez,
possibly the only person who really cares about Madame Meursault's death, ironically cannot move quickly enough to stay with
her coffin. His inability to keep up with the funeral procession—to
act in accordance with his feelings—frustrates him to the point of
tears. A third inexplicable occurrence is the scheduling of Meursault's trial just before the trial of a son who killed his father. The
prosecutor argues that Meursault's crime opened the door for the
crime of parricide, using the random circumstance of the trial schedule to help secure Meursault's death sentence. Had the two cases not
been scheduled back-to-back, Meursault might have received a
lighter sentence. Camus seems to use the extent to which each character accepts or attempts to defy the irrationality of the universe as
a signal of his or her personal worth.

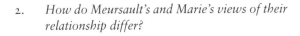

2.   *How do Meursault's and Marie's views of their*
     relationship differ?

Meursault's continual focus on Marie's body and his lack of interest in her personality show that he sees his relationship with her as purely physical. Meursault repeatedly makes comments about Marie's figure, usually noting how beautiful she looks. He describes little about their interaction other than their physical contact. The emotional aspects of their relationship are clearly secondary to Meursault. When she asks, he tells Marie that he probably does not love her, and he answers her questions about marriage with similar indifference. The fact that Marie asks these questions shows that she feels at least some emotional attachment to Meursault. At one point, she explicitly states that she loves Meursault for his peculiarities. After Meursault goes to jail, the differences between his and Marie's attitudes about their relationship become even more obvious. Whereas Marie visits Meursault and genuinely misses his companionship, Meursault only misses Marie because he misses sex. Otherwise, he hardly thinks of her.

QUESTIONS & ESSAYS

3.   *Compare Meursault to Raymond Sintes. How are the two neighbors different? How are they similar?*

At first, it seems that Raymond and Meursault could not be more different. Whereas Raymond is active and possesses a violent temper, Meursault is passive and always calm. Raymond treats his mistress cruelly, beating and abusing her, while Meursault does not seem capable of such behavior toward women. However, Raymond holds genuine feelings for his mistress and is truly hurt when he learns that she is cheating on him. Meursault, on the contrary, seems to have very little affection for Marie, whose appeal to him is predominantly physical.

Despite their differences, Meursault and Raymond hold similar positions in relation to society. Meursault's detached attitudes make him an outsider, a stranger to "normal" society. Raymond's work as a pimp brings him a similar societal stigma. Like Meursault, Raymond is on the outside of society looking in. Perhaps this similarity forms the foundation of their friendship.

SUGGESTED ESSAY TOPICS

1. Trace the development of Meursault's philosophy. How does he come to open himself to "the gentle indifference of the world"? What spurs his revelation? How do earlier events in the novel prepare us to expect it?

2. We see characters in the book solely through Meursault's eyes, but Meursault typically tells us very little. Using the information that Meursault provides, analyze a character such as Marie and Raymond. What level of insight does Meursault provide into these characters' personalities?

3. Compare and contrast the relationship between Salamano and his dog with the relationship between Meursault and his mother. What are the similarities? Which is more loving?

4. Discuss the style of *The Stranger*. How does Meursault's language correspond to the subjects he describes? Does it evolve or change as the novel goes on? Does the stripped-down prose of the novel's first half limit its expressive power?

5. Is Meursault really a threat to his society? Does he deserve the death penalty? Is he more or less dangerous than a criminal who commits a crime with clear motive?

6. In his jail cell, Meursault finds an old newspaper article about a Czechoslovakian man who is murdered by his mother and sister. How does this article relate to Meursault's own trial for murder? How does this article expand the themes in *The Stranger*? How does it support Camus's philosophy of the absurd?

7. Analyze the passages describing Meursault's walk down the beach before he kills the Arab. How does Camus build tension in the passage? How is it different from the passages preceding it? Meursault says at his trial that he killed the Arab because of the sun. Is this explanation at all valid?

REVIEW & RESOURCES

QUIZ

1. Which is Meursault's favorite place to eat lunch?

    A.   McDonald's
    B.   Chez Pierre
    C.   Marie's
    D.   Celeste's

2. Who loses his mangy dog?

    A.   Raymond
    B.   Meursault
    C.   Salamano
    D.   The caretaker

3. Who pulls out a silver crucifix when he is talking to Meursault?

    A.   The examining magistrate
    B.   The caretaker
    C.   The chaplain
    D.   The director

4. What kind of movie do Marie and Meursault see on their first date?

    A.   A drama
    B.   A documentary about Algiers
    C.   A horror movie
    D.   A comedy

5. What did the residents of the old persons' home call
    Thomas Perez when he started spending time with
    Madame Meursault?

    A. An old gigolo
    B. A leech
    C. A dirty old man
    D. Her fiancé

6. What is Meursault and Marie's favorite leisure activity?

    A. Swimming
    B. Cooking
    C. Chess
    D. Walks in the park

7. What bothers Meursault most on the day of the funeral?

    A. Thomas Perez's clothing
    B. The priest's attitude
    C. The heat
    D. The dingy church

8. What does Meursault's lawyer think of him?

    A. He admires him
    B. He seems disgusted by him
    C. He thinks he's funny
    D. He never bothers to meet him

9. Which of the following occurs first?

    A. Meursault has dinner with Raymond
    B. Salamano's dog dies
    C. Marie and Meursault sleep together
    D. Meursault's mother dies

10. What does Meursault do during the vigil for his mother?

    A. He cries all night
    B. He chats happily with Thomas Perez
    C. He smokes, drinks coffee, and sleeps
    D. He gets into a fight with the caretaker

11. Which emotion best describes Meursault's reaction to
Marie's marriage proposal?

    A.   Indifference

    B.   Fear

    C.   Elation

    D.   Disgust

12. Which person does Salamano's dog resemble?

    A.   Meursault's mother

    B.   Raymond's mistress

    C.   Meursault

    D.   Salamano

13. Which of the following people attends Meursault's trial?

    A.   Geoffrey Chaucer

    B.   Salamano's dog

    C.   Meursault's mother

    D.   Marie

14. Who is the uninvited guest that comes into Meursault's cell?

    A.   Thomas Perez

    B.   Celeste

    C.   The chaplain

    D.   The director

15. Who owns the beach house that Marie, Meursault, and
Raymond visit?

    A.   Emmanuel

    B.   Masson

    C.   Raymond

    D.   The Arab

16. What is the most damaging evidence during
Meursault's trial?

    A.   His indifference to his mother's death

    B.   Marie's testimony

    C.   Raymond's testimony

    D.   The fingerprints on the gun

17. At first, what bothers Meursault about prison?

    A. Not having cigarettes
    B. Not having sex
    C. Being cut off from nature
    D. All of the above

18. Whose gun does Meursault use to kill the Arab?

    A. Raymond's
    B. Madame Meursault's
    C. Celeste's
    D. Masson's

19. Who slaps Raymond?

    A. Meursault
    B. Salamano
    C. A policeman
    D. The chaplain

20. What method of execution will be used to kill Meursault?

    A. Guillotine
    B. Hanging
    C. Electric chair
    D. Firing squad

21. Which of these people lives in Meursault's building?

    A. Raymond
    B. Marie
    C. Celeste
    D. Thomas Perez

22. How soon after his mother's funeral does Meursault have a date with Marie?

    A. Later that afternoon
    B. A week later
    C. Exactly one year later
    D. The next day

23. What is the examining magistrate's nickname for
    Meursault?

    A. Murray
    B. Monsieur Antichrist
    C. The Beach Butcher
    D. Monsieur Heartless

24. How does Meursault feel during his lawyer's closing
    arguments?

    A. Bored
    B. Captivated
    C. Distraught
    D. Hopeful

25. Which of these is the novel's famous first line?

    A. "Another day, another dollar"
    B. "The sun shone, and again it was hot"
    C. "Maman died today"
    D. "It was the best of times, it was the worst of times"

ANSWER KEY:
1: D; 2: C; 3: A; 4: D; 5: D; 6: A; 7: C; 8: B; 9: D; 10: C;
11: A; 12: D; 13: D; 14: C; 15: B; 16: A; 17: D; 18: A; 19: C;
20: A; 21: A; 22: D; 23: B; 24: A; 25: C

Suggestion for Further Reading

BACHMAN, V. J. *Camus's Rebellious Thought.* Cahoes, New York: Talus Titles, 1999.

BLOOM, HAROLD, ed. *Albert Camus's* THE STRANGER. Philadelphia: Chelsea House, 2001.

BRONNER, STEPHEN ERIC. *Albert Camus: The Thinker, the Artist, the Man.* Danbury, Connecticut: Franklin Watts, 1996.

DAVISON, RAY. *Camus: The Challenge of Dostoevsky.* Exeter: University Press of Exeter, 1997.

ELLISON, DAVID. *Understanding Albert Camus.* Columbia, South Carolina: University of South Carolina Press, 1990.

LENZINI, JOSÉ. *Albert Camus.* Toulouse: Les Essentiels Milan, 1995.

MCBRIDE, JOSEPH. *Albert Camus: Philosopher and Litterateur.* New York: St. Martin's Press, 1992.

RIZZUTO, ANTHONY. *Camus: Love and Sexuality.* Gainesville: University Press of Florida, 1998.

WINEGARTEN, R. "Camus Today." *The New Criterion* 11.7 (1993): 35–42.

REVIEW & RESOURCES

SparkNotes Study Guides: